JOSEPHINE BAKER AND LA REVUE NÈGRE

PAUL COLIN'S LITHOGRAPHS OF *LE TUMULTE NOIR* IN PARIS, 1927

WITH AN INTRODUCTION BY HENRY LOUIS GATES, JR., AND KAREN C. C. DALTON

HARRY N. ABRAMS, INC., PUBLISHERS

In memory of Dominique de Menil

The authors wish to thank Leonard Fox and Lisina Ceresa

for obtaining for us a splendid copy of *Le Tumulte noir*, and Richard Newman for reviewing the manuscript

and allowing us to reproduce several items from his fine collection. Both the publisher and authors are grateful to

the family of Paul Colin for granting permission to reissue their ancestor's portfolio of lithographs.

EDITOR: HARRIET WHELCHEL
DESIGNER: RAYMOND P. HOOPER
RIGHTS AND REPRODUCTIONS: JOHN K. CROWLEY

Library of Congress Cataloging-in-Publication Data

Colin, Paul, 1892–1985.
Josephine Baker and La Revue nègre: Paul Colin's lithographs of
Le tumulte noir in Paris, 1927 / [new text] with an introduction by
Henry Louis Gates, Jr., and Karen C. C. Dalton.
p.   cm.
Includes bibliographical references and index.
ISBN 0–8109–2772–1 (pbk.)
1. Colin, Paul, 1892–1985. Tumulte noir.   2. Baker, Josephine,
1906–1975—Portraits.   3. Afro-American entertainers in art.
4. Afro-American entertainers—France—Paris—History—20th century.
I. Gates, Henry Louis.   II. Dalton, Karen C. C. 1948–   .
III. Title.
NE2349.5.C66A4   1998
769.92—dc21   98-10072

All works of Paul Colin © 1997 Estate of Paul Colin / Artists Rights Society (ARS), New York / ADAGP, Paris

Introduction copyright © 1998 by Henry Louis Gates, Jr., and Karen C. C. Dalton

All photographs were taken by Zindman / Fremont, New York, with the exception of the introduction photographs, as noted
in captions, and that of Rip's Preface, page 14, photographed by Boston Photo Imaging

Published in 1998 by Harry N. Abrams, Incorporated, New York
All rights reserved. No part of the contents of this book may be reproduced without the written permission of the publisher

Printed and bound in Japan

Harry N. Abrams, Inc.
100 Fifth Avenue
New York, N.Y. 10011
www.abramsbooks.com

CONTENTS

INTRODUCTION

HENRY LOUIS GATES, JR., AND KAREN C. C. DALTON

A young African-American dancer named Josephine Baker and her act, La Revue Nègre, took Paris by storm in 1925. Their arrival was trumpeted by the bold red, black, and white posters of a young French artist and set designer, Paul Colin. Colin was a brilliant caricaturist who had a way with a line. His drawings captured the spirited movements of that "wild dance," the Charleston, newly imported from the States, and the syncopated rhythms of a new art form called jazz.

In 1927, Colin created *Le Tumulte noir*,[1] a portfolio of hand-colored lithographs issued in tribute to Josephine Baker and the other African-American performers who had captivated the Parisian public during *les années folles,* those "crazy years" known in America as the Roaring Twenties. The vivid colors and vigorous lines of Colin's drawings bring to life the extraordinary talent of these musicians and dancers. Colin's dashing sketches also convey Tout-Paris's infatuation with all things black: no one is immune, from celebrities of stage and page to shopkeepers and cabdrivers. Music-hall stars Mistinguett and Maurice Chevalier Charleston frantically across the pages. A middle-aged *bourgeoise* dances until she drops like a limp cloth into an armchair; visions of an elegant black man she had seen earlier in a Montmartre nightclub dance in her head. The City of Light has fallen under the spell of black music and dance.

Paul Colin. Poster advertising Josephine Baker and La Revue Nègre at the Théâtre des Champs-Elysées, Paris. 1925. Colored lithograph, 62⅜ x 45¾" (158.4 x 116 cm). Poster Photo Archives, Posters Please Inc., New York City

Le Tumulte noir is a visual recapitulation of and homage to the Jazz Age at its peak. Its generous pages, as large as broadsides, immortalize the fortuitous encounter of two rising young talents—Baker and Colin—and their ensuing collaboration. She loved to dance; he loved to draw her dancing. Both were very good at what they did.

The sheets of *Le Tumulte noir* also suggest the communal sigh of relief African Americans exhaled in France. Arriving in significant numbers on French soil during World War I, black American soldiers experienced for the first time a society that was not organized around the principles of antiblack racial segregation and discrimination. There, segregation was illegal. Hotels, restaurants, and theaters were open to all, regardless of race. African Americans could dance all night with, and make love to, French women and men, and no one even blinked. It was not that France was innocent of racial bias: after all, its colonial rule was predicated on the presumed superiority of the French, their language, and their culture over the peoples of their African and Caribbean possessions. Nevertheless, compared to America, France was a color-blind land of tolerance. On the streets of Paris, black Americans could go about their lives without fear of running into the humiliation of Jim Crow racism just around the corner. They could become famous, like *la Joséphine*, or they could function like ordinary citizens. Above all else, they could savor the freedom of feeling like a human being for the very first time.

THE BLACKENING OF PARIS, 1900–1925

When the rage was in New York of colored people
Monsieur Siegfied of Ziegfied Follies said its geting
darker and darker on old broadway[.]
Since the La Revue Nagri came to Gai Parée
Ill say its geting darker and darker in Paris.

So wrote Josephine Baker in the epistolary preface to *Le Tumulte noir.* When she and the troupe of La Revue Nègre strolled off the Cunard liner *Berengaria* at Cherbourg on 22 September 1925, Paris was eager to receive them. The path to their success had been in preparation for some time. Since the turn of the century, a gradually swelling stream of African-American music and dance, as well as African art, particularly sculpture, had been critically acclaimed in France. The cumulative effect of the open reception to their art eventually began to alter not only how and what the French heard and saw, but also the way they *moved.*

The change began with the introduction of ragtime in Paris at the Exposition Universelle of 1900. With much fanfare, military bandleader John Philip Sousa presented this new, syncopated musical style in compositions based on the work of Scott Joplin and other African Americans. (Elsewhere at the Exposition, people from Dahomey and Senegal were on display, singing and dancing before the gawking crowds.) Two years later, at the Nouveau Cirque, African-American performers introduced to Paris a high-stepping dance companion to ragtime called the Cakewalk. This rhythmic, disjointed dance derived from a harvest "chalk-line" dance, once performed by slaves on southern plantations. The Cakewalk craze in France lasted well into the next decade, fueled by dance contests sponsored by circuses and dance halls, and by dance manuals and classes *à la* Arthur Murray.

For some, ragtime and the Cakewalk conjured up images of slaves dancing and singing on antebellum plantations in Louisiana. For others, such orgiastic, nonconventional sounds and movements transported them to some imagined West African village where "natives" and "witch doctors" did "savage," grotesque dances to pounding drums. Whether characterized as "exotic" or "savage," ragtime and the Cakewalk and their successors represented for some the capitulation of "civilization" to the "primitive" and led, many suspected, to irresponsible sexual abandon or even demonic possession.

It was indeed the liberating (or, depending on one's point of view, degenerating) effect of the so-called primitive nature of African sculpture that in 1906 attracted Henri Matisse, Pablo Picasso, and other artists then working in Paris. These members of the visual avant-garde avidly studied and, in some cases, copied Kota reliquaries, Fang masks, Bambara and Senufo figures, and other West African objects, known collectively as *l'art nègre.* They found in those sculptures new approaches to form that enabled them to reinvigorate the stifling academism of much late nineteenth-century French art. However, painters and sculptors alike were searching for more than a revolutionary formal vocabulary. They also were looking for new approaches to the process of creation. European myths held that African creative expression was spontaneous, collective, instinctive, uncensored either internally or externally, free of rules, and in touch with potent, mysterious, nonrational, and subliminal forces. Such characteristics, from the perspective of "civilized" French artists, made l'art nègre "primitive." It was that very "primitivism" they wanted to assimilate into their own work and thus transform it.

During these same years, European composers of art music, including Claude Debussy, Igor Stravinsky, and Erik Satie and the members of Les Six, began incorporating elements of ragtime and jazz in their works. Already in his 1895 article, "Music in America," the Czech composer Antonín Dvořák had recommended the use of "negro melodies" as an inspiration for a national music. In The Souls of Black Folk, published in 1903, the African-American scholar W. E. B. Du Bois espoused a similar argument for the spirituals. Many musicians and critics agreed that the regenerative force necessary to revitalize moribund European musical traditions could be found in African-American music. "Gollywog's Cakewalk" from Debussy's Children's Corner of 1906–8, Stravinsky's Le Sacre du printemps, which premiered in 1913, and Satie's score for the ballet Parade, from 1917, were among the early and significant examples of Europeans recognizing in ragtime and jazz new formal directions for their own work.

Exactly when Parisians first heard jazz is not known. Perhaps the "first" should go to drummer Louis Mitchell and his band, the Seven Spades, who played a series of jazz concerts in Paris in November 1917. The credit for popularizing jazz in France, however, must go to the segregated black regiments and their bands that began arriving in France with other American troops late in 1917. Sporting cocky names such as Harlem's Hellfighters of the 369th Regiment and Tim Brymn's Seventy Black Devils of the 350th Regiment, these U. S. Army bands gave concerts and impromptu performances all over the country. Directed by Lieutenant James Reese Europe, who had recruited musicians of the caliber of lyricist Noble Sissle, the Hellfighters made the greatest impression on Paris. In August 1918, they were sent to Paris to represent the United States at various official ceremonies celebrating the war's end. They gave a concert for the allied officers at the Théâtre des Champs-Elysées (where La Revue Nègre would open in 1925) and then overwhelmed the French public with a performance in the Tuileries Gardens. Paris went wild. According to Europe, "Everywhere we gave a concert it was a riot." Less than a year later, the same theater, as well as the Apollo Theatre in Montmartre, would present virtuoso violinist Will Marion Cook's Southern Syncopated Orchestra, fresh from a command performance before King George V at Buckingham Palace. Among this jazz orchestra's forty-one instrumentalists and nine singers was clarinetist and soprano saxophonist Sidney Bechet, a future member of La Revue Nègre.

When the armistice ending World War I was signed on 11 November 1918, about 1.4 million Frenchmen had been killed and a similar number disabled. The country was horrified at the carnage and misery it had witnessed, and deeply disturbed to realize that a continent that called itself civilized could, in fact, be so savage. Disillusioned by their own barbarity and drained by fifty-two months of horror and deprivation, the French wanted to reembrace life. Therefore, in the simplest terms, Parisians found in African-American music and dance a degree of mirth and hedonistic and voyeuristic pleasure they had not known for some time. Perhaps even more important was that the French looked to the art, music, and dance of peoples they categorized as "primitives," particularly Africans and African Americans, for ways of remaking their self-image and of defining themselves in the modern world.

JOSEPHINE BAKER: FROM SUCCÈS DE SCANDALE TO VEDETTE

While the foundations of African-American music and dance were being laid in Paris, the future "la Joséphine" unwittingly was preparing for a career as a dancer that would make her the most popular entertainer in France.

Born in the slums of East St. Louis in 1906, Josephine Baker learned from her neighbors the many steps and dances—like the Mess Around, the Itch, Trucking—that passed through America's black urban centers during the teens. Before she was fourteen, she had left home, fleeing the poverty, drudgery, and discord that went with it; married briefly, then divorced; and entered her first school of show business, the black vaudeville circuit. Following a brief stint with the three-member Jones Family Band playing trombone, doing dance routines, and making comic cross-eyed faces, Baker got her first break. She landed the role of Cupid in a love scene staged by the Dixie Steppers, a traveling troupe performing at the Booker T. Washington Theater in St. Louis. Her aerial entrance was marred by crossed wires, but her gift for comedy, even when dangling midair in distress, won the audience and the Dixie Steppers' manager.

Sussman photograph of Josephine Baker inscribed to Mr. and Mrs. Eubie Blake. 1923. Collection of Richard Newman and Belynda Bady, Boston

Too young, too small, and too skinny to be in the chorus line, young Baker accepted a job as dresser of blues singer and troupe star Clara Smith. The work was not glamorous—maintaining wardrobe, securing Miss Smith in her gauzy, undersized costumes, trying to reduce the performer's calorie intake—but it did have certain advantages. It paid nine dollars a week; it enabled Baker to leave St. Louis and travel the country from New Orleans to Philadelphia; it began teaching her the discipline required of theater work; and it revealed to her the thrill of being onstage.

By April of 1921 the Dixie Steppers were playing in Philadelphia, and Josephine Baker had risen from dresser to comic chorus girl. Demonstrating already her extraordinary energy and her evident desire to please the audience, she enlivened every show with the crazy antics and frantic dancing of the chorus girl on the end who kept forgetting the steps and messing up the routine. But Baker, like many dancers, dreamed of dancing on Broadway.

For the first time in many years, a black show was on its way to New York City. Shuffle Along—with music by Eubie Blake, lyrics by Noble Sissle, and book by Flournoy Miller and Aubrey Lyles (who later invented the characters Amos and Andy)—was to become one of the greatest musical comedies in American theater. Although the book was still mired in the conventions of minstrelsy, the music and dance broke with that racist tradition, conveying an intensity and an energy rarely if ever seen on stage. Shuffle Along was also responsible for another innovation: choreographing dances that had originated in the traditional or contemporary African-American culture and adapting them for musicals. Both the phenomenally popular Charleston and the Black Bottom were introduced to the public in this way.

Josephine Baker desperately wanted to be in the cast of Shuffle Along. During a one-night, pre-Broadway stand, she auditioned for the chorus but was rejected because she was "too young, too thin, too small, and too dark." (In New York State, chorus-line girls had to be at least sixteen years old, and Baker was not quite fifteen.) She would not be deterred. When the Dixie Steppers closed in Philadelphia, she bought a one-way ticket to New York and secured another audition for the musical. Again she was deemed "too small, too skinny." Again she was offered a job as dresser with the road company. Baker intended to refuse, but a friend advised her to accept the offer, apply herself to learning the routines, and bide her time until a chorus girl fell ill. When the opportunity to replace a member of the chorus line inevitably arrived, Josephine Baker pounced on it.

Audiences were bowled over by her frenetic dancing and outrageous clowning, the visual equivalents of malapropisms. A few years later, a critic for *Dance Magazine* described both her antics and her immense appeal:

> She was the little girl on the end. You couldn't forget her once you'd noticed her, and you couldn't escape noticing her. She was beautiful but it was never her beauty that attracted your eyes. In those days her brown body was disguised by an ordinary chorus costume. She had a trick of letting her knees fold under her, eccentric wise. And her eyes, just at the crucial moment when the music reached the climactic "he's just wild about, cannot live without, he's just wild about me" [from "I'm Just Wild About Harry"], her eyes crossed.
>
> Nothing very beautiful about a cross-eyed coloured girl. Nothing very appealing. But it was the folding knees and the cross-eyes that helped bring back the choruses for those unforgettable encores.

Word got back to Sissle and Blake that they had a sensation in the chorus line of their touring company. Every night Baker's scene-stealing antics stopped the show. When *Shuffle Along* ended its unprecedented Broadway run of more than five hundred performances, the main company went on the road. The ambitious young dancer performed in the chorus from August 1922 until the end of the tour in the fall of 1923. She was enthusiastic, outrageous, and exhilarating. Sissle and Blake worked hard to make the young performer more "professional," teaching her pacing and other skills. Their protégée mastered her lessons, as long as she was in rehearsal. Once onstage, her urge to improvise and her love of acclaim erased the carefully coached routines. Josephine Baker was a jazz artist, dancing riffs in solo improvisation.

When Sissle and Blake opened their new show *In Bamville*, later renamed and better known as *The Chocolate Dandies*, in March 1924, Josephine Baker was given star billing as "the highest paid chorus girl in the world." (She earned one hundred twenty-five dollars a week, whereas the other members of the chorus received thirty dollars.) Topsy Anna, the part created especially for Baker, was straight out of the racist minstrel tradition: she was a ragamuffin in blackface wearing bright cotton smocks and clown shoes. The poet e. e. cummings remembered her in *The Chocolate Dandies* as a "tall, vital, incomparably fluid nightmare which crossed its eyes and warped its limbs in a purely unearthly manner." The musical's "Wedding Finale," however, enabled Baker to discard her comic persona. Here she appeared as a "deserted female" dressed in a glamorous white satin gown with an alluring slit up the left leg. It was this image—the very image of an elegant, composed, polished performer—that Baker would use to conquer the French.

Baker's ticket to Paris came from Caroline Dudley Reagan, a young society woman who wanted to stage a black revue such as *Shuffle Along* or *Runnin' Wild* or *The Chocolate Dandies* in Paris. Reagan wanted to show Parisians "real" Negro music and dance. When Reagan saw Baker performing at the Plantation Club at Fiftieth Street and Broadway in the summer of 1925, she had already recruited several members of the company that would come to be known as La Revue Nègre. They included Spencer Williams, composer of "Mahogany Hall Stomp" and the more famous "Basin Street Blues"; bandleader and pianist Claude Hopkins; dancer and choreographer Louis Douglas; and set designer Miguel Covarrubias. (Born in 1904, this young Mexican artist was already making his name in New York as a caricaturist for *Vanity Fair*. His reputation was enhanced further by the publication of his *Negro Drawings* in 1927. Like *Le Tumulte noir*, which appeared the same year, Covarrubias spotlighted the energy of black dance.) To this talented group, Reagan

Miguel Covarrubias. Jazz Baby, *from* Negro Drawings. *1927 (drawing first published in* Vanity Fair, *December 1924). Collection of Richard Newman and Belynda Bady, Boston*

Photograph of the musicians of La Revue Nègre and Josephine Baker rehearsing in Paris. 1925. Courtesy of Bryan Hammond's private collection

added the musicians whom Hopkins would lead: Joe Hayman on saxophone, Daniel Day on trombone, Bass Hill on tuba, Percy Johnson on drums, and Sidney Bechet on clarinet. After some salary negotiations, Josephine Baker joined the troupe as lead dancer, singer, and comic. Rehearsals began in New York and continued on board the *Berengaria* during the crossing. By the time they reached Paris, opening night, scheduled for 2 October 1925 at the Théâtre des Champs-Elysées, was ten days away. During that brief time the revue would be transformed from a vaudeville show, replete with stereotypes and conceived for a white American public raised on segregation and racism, into a music-hall performance tailored for openly curious, somewhat voyeuristic Parisians.

Four men set to work on the transformation: the theater's forward-thinking director, Rolf de Maré; his artistic director, André Daven; the resident producer at the Casino de Paris, Jacques Charles; and the young illustrator Paul Colin. Immediately, Maré and Daven commissioned Colin to create the tricolored poster (see page 4) that would make Josephine Baker and La Revue Nègre such familiar visages all over Paris. Daven then turned to Jacques Charles to revise the revue's program to make it more "African," placing less emphasis on tap dancing and spirituals and more on Josephine Baker and her phenomenal ability to dance suggestively. To partner Baker they hired Joe Alex, a dancer, possibly from Martinique, who frequented Le Grand Duc. Le Grand Duc was a black club in Montmartre where Harlem entertainer Bricktop sang, expatriates F. Scott and Zelda Fitzgerald drank champagne, and poet Langston Hughes briefly made a living washing

White Studio photographs of Josephine Baker in costume (top) and with fellow cast members Lew Payton and Johnny Hudgins (above) in Noble Sissle and Eubie Blake's show The Chocolate Dandies. *1924. Billy Rose Theater Collection, The New York Public Library of the Performing Arts*

dishes. The "Danse sauvage" choreographed for Baker and Alex was slightly comic and highly erotic: scanty costumes consisting primarily of feathers, suggestive movements, and "jungle music" dramatically aided them in eroticizing their glistening brown bodies.

On opening night the house was packed by the time the musicians took their places: they sat on one side of the stage in front of a curtain depicting a black man dancing on a checkerboard floor. After the orchestra's first number, the curtain opened onto a Mississippi River dock scene with the company's twenty-five performers onstage, strolling, chatting, singing, dancing. Their brightly colored costumes were as dazzling as the entertainers were exotic. Few Parisians had ever seen so many black people together. When audience excitement and anticipation climaxed, Josephine Baker entered the *tableau* in blackface lips, wearing plaid dungarees, with knees bent, feet spread apart, buttocks thrust out, stomach sucked in, cheeks puffed out, eyes crossed. She appeared to be part animal—Colin saw a kangaroo, others a giraffe—part human. Her movements were just as astonishing: shaking, shimmying, writhing like a snake, contorting her torso, all this while emitting strange, high-pitched noises. Then, almost before the audience could comprehend what this apparition might possibly be, she burst offstage on all fours, stiff-legged, *derrière* extended into the air, hands spanking the boards as she scuttled into the wings.

Eight more *tableaux* followed—including a clarinet solo by Sidney Bechet in the role of a peanut vendor; a "Louisiana Camp Meeting" with Baker and Maud de Forest as brides competing for the same man; and a rapid-fire tap dance by Louis Douglas. Then came the spectacular finale, set in a Harlem nightclub. Ultimately, the stage belonged to Josephine Baker and Joe Alex and their "Danse sauvage," before which all else had been prelude. Their unforgettable entrance was seared into Janet Flanner's mind's eye. Later, she recalled:

Photograph of Josephine Baker and Joe Alex in "Danse sauvage," performed with La Revue Nègre at the Théâtre des Champs-Elysées. October 1925. Courtesy of Bryan Hammond's private collection

> She made her entry entirely nude except for a pink flamingo feather between her limbs; she was being carried upside down and doing the split on the shoulder of a black giant. Midstage, he paused, and with his long fingers holding her basket-wise around the waist, swung her in a slow cartwheel to the stage floor, where she stood like his magnificent discarded burden, in an instant of complete silence. She was an unforgettable female ebony statue. A scream of salutation spread through the theater. Whatever happened next was unimportant. The two specific elements had been established and were unforgettable—her magnificent dark body, a new model that to the French proved for the first time that black was beautiful, and the acute response of the white masculine public in the capital of hedonism of all Europe—Paris.

Another commentator, the French dance critic André Levinson, articulated not only the French male response to the "black Venus" but also the inseparability of the music and dance that characterized the performance:

> There seemed to emanate from her violently shuddering body, her bold dislocations, her springing movements, a gushing stream of rhythm. It was she who led the spellbound drummer and the fascinated saxophonist in the harsh rhythm of the "blues." It was as though the jazz, catching on the wing the vibrations of this body, was interpreting word by word its fantastic monologue. The music is born from the dance, and what a dance! The gyrations of this cynical yet merry mountebank, the good-natured

grin on her large mouth, suddenly give way to visions from which good humor is entirely absent. In the short *pas de deux* of the savages, which came as the finale of La Revue Nègre, there was a wild splendor and magnificent animality. Certain of Miss Baker's poses, back arched, haunches protruding, arms entwined and uplifted in a phallic symbol, had the compelling potency of the finest examples of Negro sculpture. The plastic sense of a race of sculptors came to life and the frenzy of African Eros swept over the audience. It was no longer a grotesque dancing girl who stood before them, but the black Venus that haunted Baudelaire.

When the curtain fell, some applauded wildly, others booed in derision, just as the first audience to hear *Le Sacre du printemps* had done in the same theater in 1913. But defenders and detractors alike shared one reaction: shock. No one had ever witnessed such unbridled sexuality on a stage. Words like *lubricity, instinct, primitive life force, savage, exotic, bestiality,* and that particularly loaded word, *degenerate,* raced through the capital. It seemed that the fragile veneer called civilization had been peeled back, revealing a primitive, protohuman core.

Exactly what this meant was the subject of fervent debate both in cafés and in the press. For some, Josephine Baker's La Revue Nègre embodied a transfusion of new blood and energy for a France stultified by tradition and sorely in need of renewal. For others, who held that the future of civilization itself lay in protecting an untainted French culture from invaders from the jungle, La Revue Nègre foretold the disintegration of centuries of classical cultural attainment, achievements of the mind over the body. Robert de Flers, member of the Académie française and prestigious reviewer for the influential daily newspaper *Le Figaro,* perceived the threat as being even more dire. According to him, the show was a "lamentable [example of] transatlantic exhibitionism which makes us revert to the ape in less time than it took to descend from it." Predictably, all this talk boosted box-office receipts at the Théâtre des Champs-Elysées and guaranteed that the Revue would be a success—the irresistible *succès de scandale* that it quickly turned out to be.

Josephine Baker's personal success was formidable. If she resembled some bizarre form of wild animal onstage, on the street she was a model of Parisian chic in designer Paul Poiret's dresses, with her well-oiled hair hugging her skull. Often escorted by Paul Colin, who sketched her in his studio as frequently as possible, Baker was invited to all the best parties in the city. Soon, she received an offer from the Folies-Bergère to be the star of their new show, "La Folie du jour" ("Madness of the Day"). Within a year, there would be Josephine Baker dolls, costumes, perfumes, and even a hairdressing called Bakerfix.

"La Folie du jour" marked *la Joséphine*'s first appearance in that venerable French institution, the Folies-Bergère. First of the French music halls, the Folies was founded in 1869. Its reputation rested on its history of presenting first-rate, popular artists (such as Yvette Guilbert, Maurice Chevalier, and Mistinguett), on elaborate sets and costumes, and, since 1894, on nudity. Nudity meant women bare from the waist up standing, like statues, in *tableaux.* The contrast between their collective alabaster immobility and Baker's dynamic mobility on opening night in April 1926 was as dramatic as Picasso's use of African masks in *Les Demoiselles d'Avignon* had been nearly twenty years earlier.

The Folies-Bergère was under the direction of a former stagehand and vaudevillian, Paul Derval. Derval had mastered the art of preparing the audience to anticipate the nudity as well as the star's (*la vedette*'s) eventual appearance. The forty-minute warmup of "La Folie du jour" established the show's theme: the refined appeal of "culture" versus the seductive allure of "nature." In eight *tableaux* about Parisian shopwindows, eight scantily clad girls representing Americans in Paris stood onstage as the wealth of Paris was displayed before them. Each chose from the bounty of elegant clothing and luxury goods, each shopper selecting fashionable clothes over Nature's finery and each leaving the stage more elegantly, and certainly more fully, dressed than when she arrived. Baker's entrance reverses this recapitulation of human cultural evolution. As e. e. cummings put it:

> She enters through a dense electric twilight, walking backwards on hands and feet, legs and arms stiff, down a huge jungle tree—as a creature neither infrahuman nor superhuman but somehow both: a mysterious unkillable Something, equally non-primitive and uncivilized, or beyond time in the sense that emotion is beyond arithmetic.

Valéry Studio photographs of Josephine Baker wearing the banana-skirt costume for "La Folie du jour" at the Folies-Bergère, Paris. April 1926. Courtesy of Bryan Hammond's private collection

And so Baker appeared onstage as the young savage Fatou, in an African jungle, with a French explorer asleep at the base of the palm tree and quasi-naked black men singing and drumming softly nearby. There she stood, laughing, in the witty, scandalous costume that would make people snicker and nudge each other for years: a girdle of drooping bananas just waiting to be aroused.

And arouse them *la Joséphine* did. Exuding bemused innuendo, her hips and stomach forced the flaccid phalluses to bounce, the bananas eventually swinging in 180-degree arcs while a gleeful Baker smiled and laughed. "This girl," wrote critic André Rouverge for the *Mercure de France*,

> has the genius to let the body make fun of itself. Her movements, while making a strikingly original rhythmic structure, go from one extreme to the other. What we would call "soul" or sensation is banished. To be sure, her body shakes as if in a trance, but with such remarkable humor. . . . The tango takes on a burlesque element and the Charleston, as danced à la Baker, fairly boils over with diabolic intensity.

Baker performed the "diabolic" Charleston that Rouverge mentions in the show's final act. From the flies overhead, an egg-shaped mass of flowers descended, opening its petals as it approached the stage and revealing therein Josephine, in a silk fringe skirt, prostrate on a mirror. Bursting forth from the egg-flower into a version of the Charleston unknown to the stage, a flurry of gleaming flesh and fringe, multiplied by the mirror's reflections and the shadows speeding about the theater, Baker seemed to be a goddess of vitality, Eros itself in blackface.

For the next years, *la Joséphine* captured the sexual imagination of Paris as few others had done. At the age of nineteen she was already a true *vedette*. She was at once erotic and comic, suggestive and playful, intense and insouciant, primitive and civilized. She embodied both the energy of *le jazz hot* and the elegance of the black

Venus. It is the certain tension between these two impulses, plus the spellbinding effect Josephine Baker had on Paris, that Paul Colin celebrates in *Le Tumulte noir*.

PAUL COLIN: MAGICIAN OF *LES ANNÉES FOLLES*

Paul Colin, c. 1930. Poster Photo Archives, Posters Please Inc., New York City

Paul Colin's beginnings, if less humble than those of Josephine Baker, were nonetheless modest. He was born 27 June 1892, in Nancy, 180 miles east of Paris, the son of a government worker. *Père* Colin assumed his son would select a similarly secure, if uninspired, future. The child's early passion for drawing, however, was a sign that his father's assumption might be mistaken.

At the age of fifteen, Paul went against his father's wishes and apprenticed himself to a printer. Three years later he enrolled in the Ecole des Beaux-Arts. Firmly convinced that starvation was the defining characteristic of an artist's life, the concerned father persuaded his son at least to be practical enough to study architecture. An observant professor quickly noticed the young man's talent and had him transferred to painting classes.

In 1912 Colin set off to make his mark in Paris; however, the capital had little need for yet another ambitious young painter. As Colin could find no regular work, the next two years were altogether bleak financially. It appeared for a time that the father's misgivings were well founded. But Colin's existence as a starving artist was to be short lived. In 1914 World War I erupted, and the struggling painter from Nancy, along with all able-bodied Frenchmen, was drafted into the military. Having seen action on battlefields from Verdun to Villers-Cotterêts, Colin was discharged four years later with a *croix de guerre* for distinguished service during the war and the rank of *maréchal des logis* (sergeant).

This time Colin's fortunes in Paris improved. Almost immediately, thanks to a friend, he received a commission to paint a mural. With his earnings he rented studio space and went to work as a painter while maintaining his "day job" as an illustrator for several small Parisian publications. In October of 1922, Colin sent twenty-five of his new paintings to an exhibition in Nancy. All twenty-five sold, a sign of very good things to come.

A chance meeting on the streets of Paris in 1923 changed Colin's life, just as Josephine Baker's unsuccessful audition for *Shuffle Along* changed hers. The person Colin encountered was a mate from his war days who was now coproducer at the Théâtre des Champs-Elysées, André Daven. Daven reported that the failing theater was about to be bought and transformed into a music hall by Rolf de Maré, radical intellectual and patron of the performing arts. In pursuit of genuine innovation in entertainment, Maré had already collaborated with avant-garde creators such as Dadaist artist Francis Picabia, composer and member of *Les Six* Georges Auric, American photographer Man Ray, inventor of the "ready-made" Marcel Duchamp, filmmaker René Clair, and star of the Swedish Ballet and choreographer Jean Borlin. For Maré's new undertaking, Daven was recruiting set and costume designers and, to publicize the theater's attractions, poster artists. Despite Colin's ignorance of the entertainment world, Daven hired him. In accepting, Paul Colin entered a milieu of daring creativity that guaranteed his transformation from an obscure artist to a celebrity.

Colin's first assignment was to design a poster for the film *Le Voyage imaginaire*, which was released in Paris in the summer of 1925 with Maré's companion Jean Borlin in the starring role. In addition,

Colin produced two posters featuring individual actors in the film, the lead Borlin and a pretty actress with a minor role, Yvonne Legeay. In these the first of numerous "vanity" posters, Colin revealed his exceptional ability to create easily identifiable portraits without resorting to a slavish rendering of the model's features. Rather, he isolated a star's salient characteristics and, without pushing to caricature, accentuated them. The resulting posters, as actors and other entertainers grasped immediately, were more valuable than portraits for publicity purposes because the simplified images were more readily recognizable. Colin's talent for formulating a visual shorthand to communicate an individual's personality would serve him well in Le Tumulte noir.

Colin's posters for Le Voyage imaginaire were significant for other reasons. They launched him into a period of feverish creativity: every month he not only generated four original posters to publicize coming attractions at the Théâtre des Champs-Elysées, but he also designed stage sets for theater and music-hall productions. This immersion in the theater was fundamental in shaping his career, just as Maré's second assignment—to devise a promotional poster for La Revue Nègre—was decisive in broadcasting his abilities and in establishing his reputation. Further, and not insignificantly, this undertaking had a transforming effect on Colin as an artist.

Colin's first passes at the Revue advertisement were crude. The only blacks he had ever seen were African and West Indian immigrant workers. Consequently, his first sketches owed more to the received stereotypes of minstrel-show imagery than to firsthand observation. At least two encounters contributed to modifying his vision. First, Colin must have seen some of the caricatures by Miguel Covarrubias of "The New Negro, a Distinctive Type Recently Created by the Coloured Cabaret Belt in New York." These lively drawings of Harlem blacks, which appeared in the December 1924 issue of Vanity Fair, included a young woman dancing in a short dress (see page 6). This figure, only slightly modified, represented Josephine in Colin's Revue Nègre poster.

The second, and ultimately more important, encounter occurred when Colin actually saw Josephine Baker and La Revue Nègre perform. He recalled that moment some thirty years later in his autobiography, La Croûte (1957):

The black troupe which arrived from Le Havre rehearsed for the first time one October morning in 1925. Rolf de Maré and André Daven had the curtain raised and the house lit earlier than usual. Just out of the wings, without even acknowledging the balconies, there were only shrieks and leaps. The symbolic figures in Maurice Denis's frescoes,[2] which crowned Auguste Perret's architecture, seemed to stiffen at the sight of this black tumult. Angels and muses flinched in indignation. Celestial harpists reacted in visible horror to the clattering sound of tap shoes. A generation separated violin melodies from the possessed uproar of clarinets and saxes.
Harlem on the Champs-Elysées! Harlem with its contortions, its howls, its multicolored feathers against coal black skin, its banner of trembling or hardened buttocks, its pairs of provocative, yielding, athletic, jolly breasts! Harlem, with its starched shirt fronts, its cotton fabrics, its boaters, its gray bowler hats, its pomaded hairdos, and its odors, exported to Europe for the first time the Charleston.

Regarding his first glimpse of Josephine Baker, Colin's recollections were vivid:

Dressed in rags, she was part boxer kangaroo, part rubber woman, part female Tarzan. She contorted her limbs and body, crossed her eyes, shimmied, puffed out her cheeks, and crossed the stage on all fours, her kinetic rear end becoming the mobile center of her outlandish maneuvers. Then, naked but for green feathers about her hips, her skull lacquered black, she provoked both anger and enthusiasm. Her quivering belly and thighs looked like a call to lubricity, like a magical return to the mores of the first ages. I still see her, frenzied, undulating, moved by the saxophones' wail. Did her South Carolina dances foretell the era of a new civilization, finally relieved of fetters centuries old?

Colin was astonished and inspired by what he saw. He remarked that "these Negroes made use of elementary means to achieve astonishing results in which the purest, because the most instinctive, artistic feeling comes through free of all constraints." And he added in parenthetical explanation: "The same thing makes for the interest and disconcerting beauty of the famous Douanier [Henri] Rousseau's paintings."

Despite his inexperience, Colin understood almost instinctively that a poster could not express the kaleidoscope of impressions and sensations he had received from Josephine Baker and La Revue Nègre. To be effective it had to communicate a single, strong idea. It had to embody the essence of the uncanny. Explaining the art of poster design to his students some years later, he emphasized that a poster's message must be comprehensible "at 100 kilometers an hour." He said they should not expect to discover the idea for a poster in their pencil lead. Rather it had to "flower" from the poster's subject. According to Colin, the creation of a poster begins with an "astonishing idea, an unexpected graphic solution which itself must be on the cutting edge of artistic movements." In his succinct words: "A poster is first and foremost a signal."

Applied to the troupe from Harlem, Colin's concepts about poster design resulted in an image that excited all of Paris, an image that launched the careers of both Josephine Baker and Paul Colin. Three bold colors: black, red, and white. Three figures: Josephine Baker—hair slicked back, arms akimbo, dancing the Charleston—in the limelit apex of a pyramid completed by a black musician in tuxedo and a black tap dancer in bowler hat. Big red lips; big black and white eyes, hers like olives, theirs like parking meters: features often used to make blacks look bewildered and bestial, here make the entertainers appear alert, spirited, "with-it." One clear idea reinforced by expressive typography: energetic, rhythmic, boldly new entertainers have arrived. Paris took to the idea at once.

Both before and after Colin designed the Revue Nègre poster, he drew numerous sketches of Josephine Baker nude. The artist's perhaps apocryphal description of Baker's first visit to his studio has a familiar ring of Gallic bravado: "She appeared in an unbelievable get-up—red dress, green shoes, aigrettes on her head. Anyone will understand the first thing I did: I undressed her."

Josephine's recollections of that first posing session are, not surprisingly, quite different. She scarcely knew Colin, having met him only a few hours earlier at the troupe's first open rehearsal. She was unaccustomed to posing at all for anyone, and certainly not without her clothes. Since neither spoke or understood the other's language, Colin communicated via small drawings. She got the picture: he

Paul Colin. Five sketches of Josephine Baker, from Les Mémoires de Josephine Baker. 1927. Collection of Richard Newman and Belynda Bady, Boston

wanted her to disrobe. She refused. But, as he sketched her, she relaxed under his scrutinizing eye and found herself more at ease in her own skin, until, as she recounted in her fifth and final autobiography:

> At a stroke I lost my uncertainty. Perhaps it dropped away with my slip. It's difficult to analyse it all. . . . Every day I became merrier with M. Colin. I called him Paul. But men are strange, they rarely understand the feelings that they bring forth in others. I loved his company, usually silent, and the time spent in the calm of his studio. He took me to the theater, brought me back to my hotel; he gave me confidence. Under his eyes, for the first time in my life I felt beautiful.

Several of Colin's sketches of Josephine appeared as illustrations in her first autobiography, *Les Mémoires de Joséphine Baker*, published in 1927, the same year as *Le Tumulte noir*. To say that Josephine "posed" for these drawings seems to be a contradiction, for each explodes with movement. They have more in common with stop-action frames than with traditional studio sketches. Judging from their extraordinary sense of spontaneity, not from any imprecision in the drawing, Colin must have dashed off some of them in a matter of seconds. Others, which were worked up into key plates for *Le Tumulte noir*, resulted from longer studies. But even those speak of movement, not stasis.

One suspects that, in fact, Josephine rarely "posed" for Paul Colin. One suspects she danced for him. That is the central idea of Colin's drawings: the dance, and more specifically, Josephine Baker dancing. His vigorous lines freeze her flexed wrists and planted feet, her angular elbows and bent knees, her strong thighs and mobile pelvis, her supple back and saucy rump, elastic arms and endless legs, the constantly alternating contractions and extensions, the sustained energy of a knowing body drawing a line in space and making it live beyond the end of the beat. Josephine Baker loved to dance. In 1927 she told one of her biographers, Marcel Sauvage, prophetically: "I shall dance all my life, I was born to dance, just for that. To live is to dance, I would like to die, breathless, spent, at the end of a dance." (Her death came, as she wished, during her afternoon nap the day after her final triumphant performance in Paris on 9 April 1975.) It is hardly surprising that Paul Colin loved to draw her in performance.

LE TUMULTE NOIR: THE PORTFOLIO

*L*e Tumulte noir is a portfolio of forty-five hand-colored lithographs published in January 1927 by Editions d'Art "Succès" of Paris. Each page measures 18½ x 12½ inches. Henri Chachoin, a printer Colin often used until the mid-1930s, ran an edition of five hundred unnumbered copies, on wove paper, and twenty numbered copies, ten on Japan paper and ten on Madagascar paper. Paul Colin drew the images onto the lithographic stones, and J. Saudé stenciled in the color. The complete edition sold out from one day to the next. The Paris press called it a masterful work. Many still consider *Le Tumulte noir* to be Colin's masterwork.

The title page of *Le Tumulte noir* sets the tone for the entire portfolio.[3] Like the poster for La Revue Nègre, the page has only three colors: black, red, and white. Boxy, childlike black letters, punctuated with two red ones, threaten to burst off the white page. They refuse to sit on the baseline in an orderly fashion, some leaning this way, others rocking that way, too full of energy to stay still. The words *tumulte* and *noir* march off in different directions, creating a shape like the bell of a trumpet blowing a fanfare for what is to follow and inviting us to be drawn into *Le Tumulte noir*.

Two prefaces prepare the reader for the drawings inside. The first is signed by Rip, the *nom de plume* of Georges Thenon (1886–1941), author of more than one hundred musical revues and one of the great satirists of the period. Rip recognized Colin's talent early on, placed his own considerable reputation behind advancing the young artist's career, and engaged him to design sets and costumes

for many of his own productions. Rip's preface turns a mocking eye on Paris in the grip of a Charleston epidemic.[4] The city has succumbed to the *tumulte noir*. According to Rip, some Negroes in Africa, whose ancestors were slaves in America, decided in turn to enslave Europe. Arriving with no more than an extra shirt and a saxophone, the invaders completely overwhelmed Paris. Since that time, Rip comments mordantly: "We have adopted their customs, we learned their dances. We have vied at Negrifying ourselves." Everywhere he turns he sees "Negro dances, Negro bands, Negro festivals, Negro balls, and exhibitions of Negro art." The peak of the craze, Rip diagnoses, was the "appearance of the great *Joséphine*'s frenetic derrière," and the dance known as the Black Bottom signaled the final phase of the campaign. The epidemic has run its course, and the city is beginning to recover its equilibrium. Rip maintains that Paul Colin and his posters should not be held responsible for the city's temporary lunacy. However, surely the artist was correct to set his penetrating eye and sure hand to recording for posterity the period of "national craziness" known as *le tumulte noir*.

The second preface is by Josephine Baker herself and is in her own handwriting. Josephine's preface confirms Rip's satirical analysis of Paris's total infatuation with "colored people" and especially with "the Charleston, that mad dance." She jokes about domestic disputes over the "right way" to do the Charleston, and traffic jams precipitated by a driver encouraging his horse with the words that also signaled passersby to begin the Charleston, "Hey, Hey!" She also hints with a wink that even hanky-panky at the office has been replaced by the Charleston.

Both prefaces direct the reader's attention to the two principal subjects of *Le Tumulte noir*: the relatively recent arrival of Josephine Baker and La Revue Nègre on the Paris scene, and their wildly enthusiastic reception by the Parisian public. In fact, the portfolio is loosely divided along similar lines into two sections. The first nineteen lithographs expose the intoxicating and liberating effect *le tumulte noir* had on Tout-Paris, particularly on the theater and music-hall celebrities of the day. The next five drawings form a transition section centered on Josephine Baker. The remaining plates focus on all the black performers who created *le tumulte noir*, presenting them both on stage and in the tiny, jumping nightclubs in Montmartre where they congregated to party after performances.

A flashback of a night out on the town is the metaphor Colin used to link the lithographs in *Le Tumulte noir* into a coherent narrative. The portfolio opens with the drawing of a middle-aged, middle-class woman (pl. 1)—we will call her Madame Bourgeoise—who reappears several times in the album. She represents the mobs of ordinary Parisians, both female and male, who were seduced by *le jazz hot* and by the exotic black performers in La Revue Nègre. Still wearing her claret cocktail dress after attending a performance at the music hall followed by dancing at a cabaret, she collapses into a comfortable chair and dreams about her evening. Her first recollection (pl. 2) is of a tall black man in an elegant dinner jacket dancing a tango with a pink-skinned woman in a low-backed dress. Charged Copenhagen blue outlines bind the couple into a single form and set them off against the mirror in the background. In the mirror the man's head is transformed into a skull, perhaps reflecting an underlying ambivalence Madame Bourgeoise feels about this attractive but alien presence. Or perhaps she recalls the medieval European associations between blackness and death.

The next image shifts the spotlight onto the Parisian celebrities themselves. Time has swallowed up the significance of many of these performers for us, as well as some of their personal quirks and habits, which are caught by the caricaturist's pen. Yet in their day they dominated the stage. This is the world Paul Colin lived, breathed, and observed. All these entertainers have fallen under the spell of the Charleston and *le tumulte noir*. In his preface Rip accused Parisians of undergoing "heliotherapy" (sunlight treatment) to "transform their white skin into boiled leather," and the dark skin color of all these popular idols would seem to confirm his statement. Further, each of them is either executing some frantic dance step or has been "Africanized" in some way. One famous person after another is caricatured, some less gently than others.

Well-known actress Jane Marnac (1886–1976) is the first to take the stage (pl. 3), in the rain (a reference to her role in *Pluie*). She laughs and flings her legs in her version of the "wild" dance while the fuchsia feathers in her hair, her short tangerine dress, and pomegranate umbrella reinforce the energetic lines of her body. She was the first partner of renowned music-hall singer Maurice Chevalier (1888–1972), who appears on the facing page (pl. 4). The ever suave, ever debonair Chevalier, with boater and cane, collapses his knees inward à *la* Josephine Baker, twists his hips, and flips his wrist to some rhythmic melody we can only imagine. A cool blue brushstroke streaks up his elongated leg and reappears beside his broad torso.

Colin's sleek drawing (pl. 5) of Damia, stage name of singer and cabaret artist Maryse Damien, is a visual pun on her signature costume, a V-necked, sleeveless black sheath that emphasized her pale white skin. Here, as in a photographic negative, her black skin and hair contrast with her white dress as a young black sailor watches her perform. Damia's cool elegance is set off against the eager athleticism of Suzanne Lenglen (1899–1938), champion French tennis player who dangles and dances in halter top and shorts on plate 6.

It is as though Colin has staged a spectacular, imaginary opening night attended by everyone who is anyone in the Paris entertainment world. (In fact, this gala on paper is not unlike the *Bal nègre* Colin threw at the Théâtre des Champs-Elysées in February 1927, one month after the publication of *Le Tumulte noir*. The invited guests came costumed and made up as their favorite black performer or musician living in Paris.) Cécile Sorel (born 1873), celebrated actress of the Comédie-Française, sweeps in on a sea of beribboned tulle like a topless Marie-Antoinette with her shepherdess's crook (pl. 7). Georges Goursat (1863–1934), whose caricatures of theater people, writers, and the upper class were all signed Sem, is transformed into a bespectacled monkey whose every limb and appendage are in the swing (pl. 8). It appears that Sem—French spelling of Shem, Noah's oldest and favorite son, and supposedly father of one of the three human races—has so fallen under the spell of the black craze that he has fulfilled the naysayers' prophecy and regressed to a simian state.

Meanwhile, film star Spinelly (née Andrée Faurier, 1890–1966), standing on a checkerboard floor, is a Joséphine look-alike, with her brown body, arched back, perky breast, and boldly patterned loincloth (pl. 9). Singer, playwright, and radio personality Saint Granier is reduced to a smiling theatrical mask on the same plate (pl. 10) as Nikita Balieff, who waggles his index finger in the air and dances in front of a pair of Senegalese soldiers. Parysis is transmogrified into an African sculpture perched atop a cane (pl. 11), while ballet dancer Jean Borlin in tux and top hat waves a Swedish flag and struts a Cubist rag (pl. 12).

Maud Loty displays her black bottom and throws a wide-eyed glance at the audience (pl. 13), but Gabriel Signoret (1878–1937), actor of stage and screen noted for his portrayal of risible old men, ignores her antics (pl. 14). Rendered as a mask on a sculpture stand, presumably to recall the many African masks then visible in Paris shops, Signoret turns away from a bare behind only to encounter something even more shocking on the following page. A totally nude and ecstatic Ida Rubenstein (1880–1960) does rubber legs under a palm tree with sherbet green fronds (pl. 15). Rubenstein was a Russian dancer, mime, and patron of the arts (she commissioned Ravel's *Bolero*) whom imperial censors in Saint Petersburg had forbidden to perform Michel Fokine's solo called *Salome* in the early 1900s.

Ida's is a tough act to follow, but Max Dearly (born Max Rolland, 1874–1943) does his best (pl. 16). This experienced music-hall performer, who partnered the incomparable Mistinguett, and film actor appears as a monocled dandy in checked trousers and a butterfly bow tie, shirtless, his pocket watch dangling where his vest pocket should

be. He strikes a familiar Josephine Baker pose, cocking one leg and straightening the other to push back his rump as his bent-elbowed arms and waving wrists dance above him. Ever popular in Parisian music halls, the twin Dolly Sisters, Rosika and Yansci (pl. 17), in towering green feather headdresses and revealing feather skirts, march across the stage like good chorus girls. Finally, Mistinguett (née Jeanne Bourgeois, 1875–1956), the most idolized of all the music-hall performers present (pl. 18), makes her appearance, and a rather surprising one it is. In her typical entrance at the Folies-Bergère, Mistinguett donned a shimmering sheath with a long train, an elaborate headdress, and a fan-shaped tailpiece of plumes, and majestically descended a vertiginous stairway to meet her clamoring fans. Yet here, she too is overcome by the *tumulte noir*. Baring her legs and her bosoms, she cloaks herself in flapper beads and dances to gleeful excess.

The parade of besotted stars comes to an end with the person who announced them in the beginning, Rip (pl. 19). He, the critic, stands in the theater and watches the show. Though he too is brown-skinned and wears a bowler hat, and therefore has not totally escaped the effects of the black craze, he nonetheless has maintained some distance, some reason. And what does he see onstage? Three thick-lipped, grinning monkeys doing the cancan. The ambivalence is undeniable. Despite the very real sensation black American musicians and dancers had created in Paris, at least some French could not quite dispel lingering notions of the inherent inferiority of blacks. Although Harlem was in America, these people were black, and, in the end, the French associated blacks with Africa, and Africa with savagery and bestiality. As this simian chorus line indicates, the discredited idea that Africans were situated in the Chain of Being somewhere between orangutans and Europeans—not fully animal, not quite human—was still part of France's colonialist psyche.

Two calligraphic drawings, like the curtains on a stage, bracket three sensational plates that form the core of *Le Tumulte noir* and create the transition to the second half of the portfolio. The first word-drawing (pl. 20) represents a black man with big round eyes and a broad grin beneath a bowler hat. The words that form his features read: "These blacks inject movement. Their mouth resembles a crater that spits out slivers of glass. . . . Their eyes have brotherly pupils. Their eyes have brotherly pupils. India ink streams down their hot temples, and some say their granddaddies ate leopard. They have might in their guts. Meanwhile music is sweet in Honolulu."

The warm-up act is over. It is time for the *vedette*. The curtains part to reveal the star of the show and the era. Like a centerfold *avant la lettre*, the eager crowd finally glimpses the lithe, coffee-colored body of Josephine Baker in motion (pls. 21 and 22). Facing away from the audience and stripped of all but her notoriously brief and suggestive costumes, she re-creates the two dances that cinched her fame: the "Danse sauvage" (without partner Joe Alex) from La Revue Nègre and her solo from the revue at the Folies-Bergère. Every line trembles. The pages seem too small to contain her. Elbows and knees push aside the air to make way for the sinewy, elongated back and rounded thighs. In the center of each figure, scarcely concealed beneath the feathers and bananas, is the force field from which emanated the blurred, rhythmic pelvic movements that became an essential part of the Baker legend. Her elastic limbs are by turns aggressive, then poetic. Absent the broad smile and crossed eyes, Josephine is pure sensuality, pure dance. She is a European fantasy come true: beautiful, erotic, African, savage.

But the show must end, and with it, the fantasy. In its place (pl. 23) is a triumphant *Joséphine* in a swishy sundress and jaunty bonnet. Her feet planted far apart and her hands firmly planted on her hips, she flashes a magnetic smile and releases a raucous, and no doubt mischievous, laugh.

Closing the brackets around *la Joséphine* is a second calligraphic drawing (pl. 24) in the form of a palm tree. Its rhythmic message, written in French and a pseudo-African language, forms the tree's fronds, trunk, and base: "Sniffing the ground / and following the trail of / Koumba N'DAO / ALL of PARIS fell / into the black pot. /

Koumba N'DAO / believed Sincerely / that all men / were black, even in Paris. / Koumba N'DAO / mak anaé / Thak anaé / Mon Ri-lo-ga / all believed that / they all believed that— / yes, yes."

A high-stepping Spanish dancer (pl. 25), perhaps Vincente Escudero, of whom Colin did a poster in 1925, leads off the second section of *Le Tumulte noir* and moves from the music hall to the *boîte de nuit*. Escudero heralds a two-page chalk drawing on a blackboard (pls. 26, 27) of a jazz orchestra. The eight black musicians in tuxedos—two trumpeters, three saxophonists (alto, tenor, and bass), a tuba player, a drummer, and a trombonist—play the music that will be heard throughout the rest of the portfolio. Here, in the crowded confines of a black club in Montmartre, Colin seems less at home. He observes more as an outsider than from within. The denizens of this world, with the exception of Josephine Baker, are not really people Colin knows. In these drawings, he captures the way they move, their style. But his caricatures, rather than becoming individualized, remain generic.

Madame Bourgeoise reappears (pl. 28), minus her chair and her dress, practicing the Charleston in front of a mirror. Colin singles out from the packed dance floor four stylish couples of black men and white women (pls. 29, 31, 32, 34), completely absorbed in the music and their own syncopated movements. They dance entwined across the pages, pausing in a lunge here, revealing a pink bottom there. Our middle-aged *Parisienne*, once again in her party dress, dreams of an impossibly long-legged stepper in tails and bowler (pl. 30). Back on the dance floor, a broad-shouldered, wasp-waisted dandy in orange trousers and tie pauses to lean on his cane and size up the crowd (pl. 33).

Meanwhile on the stage, Josephine Baker on top of the piano wears a hot-pink marabou bustle and lets loose an electric Charleston, flinging her monkeylike arms to balance her lashing legs (pls. 35, 37). She is more fully clothed—red and yellow polka-dot dress, green boots, and red hat with magenta feathers—but no less kinetic in another Charleston solo (pl. 38). These frantic images contrast sharply with a drawing of a chic Josephine standing on a Parisian street corner in a fur-collared melon coat, clutching her handbag (pl. 36). Colin seems to be juxtaposing the two Josephine Bakers—the nearly nude, inventive stage performer and the glamorous, elegantly attired young woman from Harlem—although the implication is that sooner or later she will burst into exuberant dance.

The evening's mood builds to a frenzy as the effects of the music, the dance, and the alcohol take command. A strutter in tails, white gloves and spats, and wire-rimmed shades (pl. 39), who resembles the elegant presence in Madame Bourgeoise's dream, announces the finale. Trapped like a wild animal in a circus cage, behind the insistent gray bars that punctuate a two-page spread, stand Josephine Baker as a bare-breasted savage and Josephine Baker in men's clothing, both unleashing a red-hot Charleston (pls. 40, 41). With this feverish sexual fantasy, the show reaches its climax.

One last nattily dressed black dancer, two parallel S-curves defining his torso and slim hips, touches his bowler and gives us a parting glance (pl. 42). Outside the club, where Josephine Baker, the musicians, and the clubs' unflagging patrons are still visible through the open doorway, the doorman bows and bids us, "Good night" (pl. 43). On a climactic double-page spread (pl. 44), the jazz musicians, seen against a backdrop of their cruise liner from America and scenes of Paris, play one last number. Then what happens? *La Baker* (pl. 45) does one last unforgettable, kaleidoscopic Charleston.[5]

Thus ends the portfolio, its final page reserved for *la Joséphine*, the dynamic performing phenomenon from America who popularized African-American music and dance in France, and who, in doing so, became the symbol of *le tumulte noir* and of the inebriating effect the black craze had on the Parisian public. Between 1925 and 1927, when the French capital experienced a small invasion of African Americans armed with the music of jazz and the movement of the Charleston and the Black Bottom, Paris christened Josephine Baker the invaders' leader and gladly surrendered to their conquering influence.

Many Parisians welcomed this "transfusion of new blood" and the therapeutic effect they assumed it would exercise over a decadent civilization desperately in need of renewal.

This climate of openness would not last, however. Already in 1921, what became known as "The Call to Order" in postwar France had been issued, admonishing a return to French "classical" traditions and a rejection of such foreign influences as African art and African-American music and dance. Throughout Europe, resentment mounted against foreign workers taking jobs from impoverished locals struggling in weak economies. And although the National Socialist party would not come to power in Germany until 1933, the first volume of Adolf Hitler's *Mein Kampf* had already appeared in 1925. His anti-Jewish, anti-Negro (whom he called "half-apes"), anti-anything-non-Aryan ideas were circulating widely. Thus, when Baker embarked on a year-long European tour in 1928, the enthusiastic reception Paris had given her was not equaled elsewhere. In Vienna, conservative opposition called her "degenerate" and her performance "pornographic." In Budapest, the audience resented seeing so many blacks on a Hungarian stage. And in Munich, the police charged that her performance might create disturbances and corrupt public morals, and therefore banned it.

Paul Colin's *Le Tumulte noir* captures a complex intercultural moment. Through Colin's drawings, we sense the delight and disorientation that Paris experienced when it first encountered African-American music and dance in the persons of Josephine Baker and La Revue Nègre.

Josephine Baker was primitivist modernism on two legs, the Cubists' *art nègre* in naked human form. Despite its unparaled degree of acceptance of, and acclaim for, a black performer, Colin's magnificently haunting recapitulation of received primitivist simian stereotypes only underscores the partial success that art can have in the grand combat against racism.

NOTES

1. A list of possible translations of the word *tumulte* includes: uproar, commotion, tumult, turmoil, hubbub, storm, hullabaloo, turbulence, frenzy, sensation, rage, brouhaha, and craze. Thus, the title *Le Tumulte noir* conveys the energizing excitement African art and African-American music and dance injected into the French capital after World War I.

2. Frescoes by French Symbolist painter and writer Maurice Denis (1870–1943) decorate the interior of the Théâtre des Champs-Elysées. They represent the American dancer Isadora Duncan (1878–1927), barefoot, moving in her flowing tunics that resembled the clothing on classical Greek sculptures.

3. The portfolio comes in a wrapper embossed with the title as described above and Paul Colin's name. Within this wrapper is an inside wrapper printed on onionskinlike paper. The front page of this interior wrapper bears the following colophon: "Les lithographies de cet album, mises sur pierre par Paul COLIN, ont été tirées pour les Editions d'Art 'Succès,' 7, Impasse Marie-Blanche–PARIS–XVIIIe, sur les presses de Henri CHACHOIN Maitre-Imprimeur, et coloriées au patron par J. SAUDÉ sous la direction artistique de Edouard DUPONT." The text on the wrapper's back page specifies the edition size: "Il a été tiré de cet album qui ne sera jamais réédité: 10 exemplaires sur Japon numérotés de 1 à 10; 10 exemplaires sur papier de Madagascar numérotés de 11 à 20; 500 exemplaires sur papier Velin teinté des Papeteries Aussedat."

Following the two wrappers is a first title page printed as follows: "LE TUMULTE NOIR / PAR / PAUL COLIN / PRÉFACE DE RIP." Its reverse is blank. The following page has Rip's Preface on the recto and a blank verso. Similarly, Josephine Baker's letter appears on the next page, with nothing on its verso. The viewer then encounters the title typeset in the same animated typography as that used on the portfolio wrapper. On the verso of this page is the first lithograph in the portfolio.

4. A translation of Rip's preface is on page 63.

5. The dancer was misidentified as Adelaide Hall by a previous owner of the portfolio.

LE TUMULTE NOIR

par

PAUL COLIN

Je ne crois pas qu'il soit juste de tenir Paul COLIN, portraitiste attitré de l'impératrice Joséphine Baker pour responsable de l'épidémie charlestonesque — voire charentonesque — qui s'est abattue, il y a deux ans sur Paris et la grande banlieue. Au vrai, le vomito negro qui sévit dans nos murs fit son apparition bien avant que ceux-ci ne se couvrissent d'effigies à la gloire de la fameuse étoile noire. Et, dès l'armistice, les Parisiens, atteints de négropathie, commencèrent d'obéir à l'ukase de l'Oncle Tom.

Les nègres d'Afrique, dont les aïeux furent promus esclaves en Amérique, rêvèrent un jour de réduire à leur tour l'Europe en esclavage. Ils se mirent donc en route, avec pour tout bagage une chemise de rechange et un saxophone ; et, débarquant deux par deux, trois par trois, Cafre par Cafre, ils envahirent, Peul à Peul, l'ancien continent et, si nous en croyons l'Agence Havas, mirent le Cap sur Paris.

Dès lors, nous adoptâmes leurs coutumes, nous apprîmes leurs danses, nous nous négrifiâmes à qui mieux mieux.

Au bar du Chatham, devenu une succursale du Bahr-el-Ghazal, on vit des messieurs se noircir consciencieusement. Aux thés du Carl' (es) ton, on entendit des poules (de Soudan, sans doute) chuchoter mystérieusement " Ma coco ! Ma coco ".

De la Pentecôte (d'Ivoire) à la Toussaint (Louverture), ce ne fut que danses nègres, orchestres nègres, fêtes nègres, bals nègres, expositions d'art nègre.

Il y eut le salon du Congo.

A cette époque, Mr Salomon Reinach déclara Madame Jane Cheirel rigoureusement hottentote ; on se passionna pour Pola Negri ; le guide Bædecker, à l'usage des étrangers qui visitent notre capitale, fut remplacé par le guide Baker ; toutes les Parisiennes demandèrent à l'héliothérapie de transformer leur peau blanche en cuir bouilli.

Et c'est au Canni-bal de la comtesse d'Iguidi qu'on s'occupa de porter à l'Académie française un poète qui parlait petit nègre : Monsieur Paul Valéry.

L'apparition du derrière frénétique de la grande Joséphine marqua l'apogée du TUMULTE NOIR et détermina la crise finale.

Le black-bottom fut en quelque sorte le delirium tremens de la Négrite. Dieu merci, l'épidémie semble décroître. La rage tend à se localiser. Les cas de folie furieuse diminuent. Il y a moins de vieilles dames qui meurent en dansant le charleston. Les convulsionnaires de la chorégraphie tropicale sont plus rares.

Aïssaouah-toi, ça va se passer.

Paul Colin a donc eu raison de fixer pour les générations futures, cette période de maboulisme national, laïque et obligatoire. Sous son crayon incisif, scalpel à la fois et bistouri, ces planches de la Vie Parisienne de 1918 à 1928, semblent être destinées à quelque musée Dupuytren.

L'art aigu de Paul Colin, sa stylisation schématique, sous laquelle se devine une science rigoureuse du dessin, son sens incroyable du mouvement permettront aux ballerines de l'avenir de reconstituer les danses modernes, comme d'après les peintures des vases grecs, nous avons pu retrouver les pas qui furent en honneur aux Panathénées.

Et les ballerines de l'avenir seront immédiatement dirigées vers l'infirmerie spéciale du Dépôt.

Topic of the Day.

When the rage was in New York of colored people
Monsieur Ziegfied of Ziegfied Follies said its getting
darker and darker on old Broadway"
Since the da Revue Nagri "came to Gay Paree,
I'll say its getting darker and darker in Paris
In a little while it shall be so dark untill one shall
light a match then light another to see if the first
is lit are not,
As the old saying is I may be a dark horse but you'll
never be a black mare,
By the way we can't forget the "charleston" that maddance
a friend ask me to pay them a visite;
But when I went to their home, people were in front of
the house, and dogs were barking, I didn't know what to think
but on the second thought I desided to inter,
on intering the cat was hanging on the chandlier the birds cage
turned over, dishes were broken and the two people looked as
if a terrible storm had happened, of course with this sight
I did know again what to do, go in or out, but by me being
so curouis I intered, When they saw me, both stopsed
the wife saying witch is right josephine this way or that
then the husband said, no it isent I tell you this the
right way. isent it josephine!) as a matter of fact I dident
know what to say, so I ask if they would try to cool down
a bit, I would try to see, All this time I dident know what they
were talking about, on this idear they stopsed, told me they were
dancing the charleston; and to make peace in the family
I said both were right,

Its not saft to walk in the streets now,
When the driver says, "Hey" "Hey" to make his horse
stop, the people think he means "charleston" and
start Dancing's, dont stop untill each fall out and
faint.
The new way of meeting a friend

Marcel. "Hey" "Hey"
Jacky. Charleston
Marcel, Did you hear the scandle that happens
yesterday;
Jack -- Why no, What happened?
Marcel My fathers secretary and foreman
was cought in the office
Jacky doing what ????,?????
Marel The Charleston "of course idiot"
Josephine Baker

retour du music-hall

Plate 1

Plate 2

Plate 3

Maurice Chevalier

Plate 4

Damia

Plate 5

Plate 6

Plate 7

Sem.

Plate 8

Plate 9

Plate 10

Plate 11

Jean Börlin

PAUL
COLIN

Plate 12

Manus Loty

PAUL
COLIN

Plate 13

Signoret

PAUL
COLIN

Plate 14

Plate 15

Plate 16

Dolly sisters

PAUL
COLIN

Plate 17

Plate 18

Plate 19

Plate 20

Plate 21

Plate 22

Plate 23

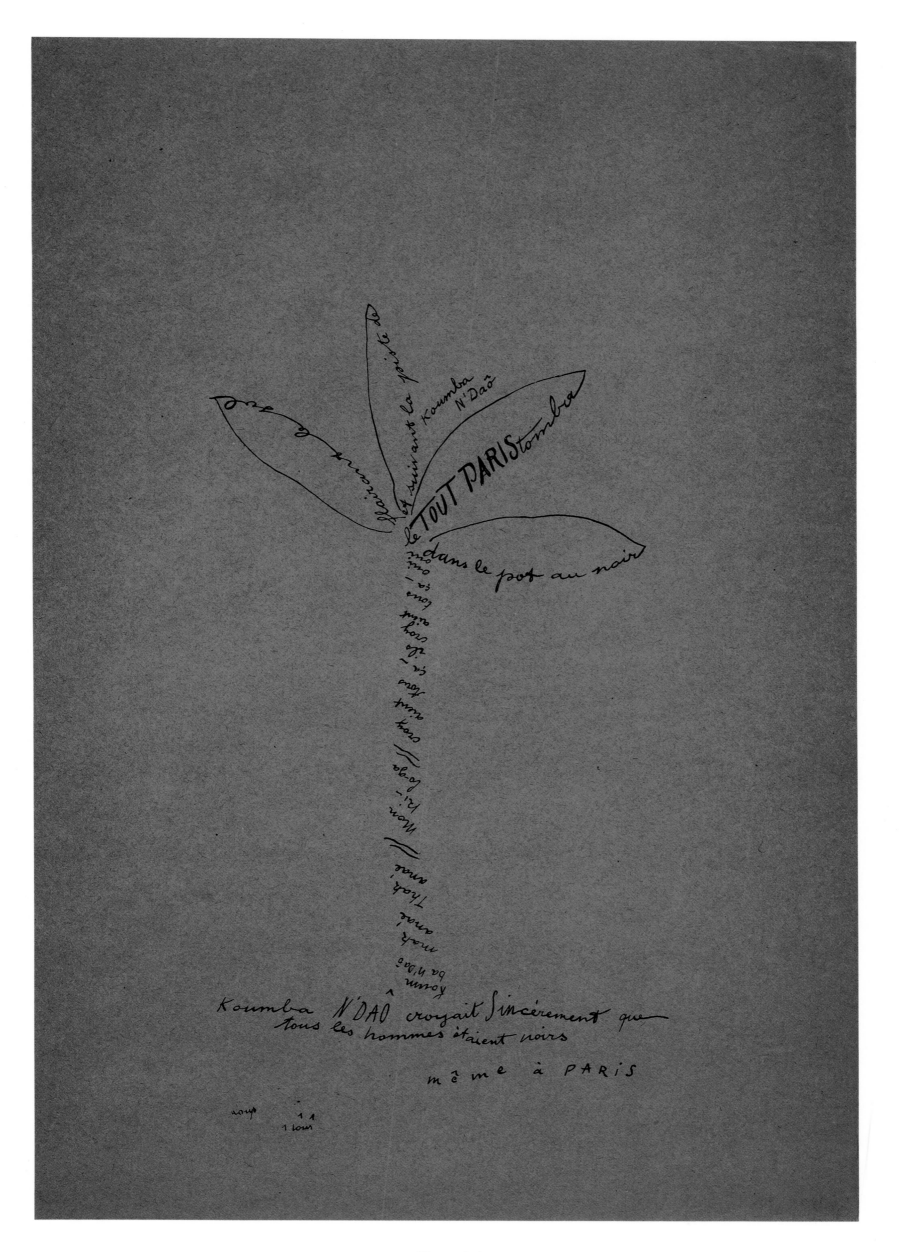

Plate 24

Plate 25

Plate 26

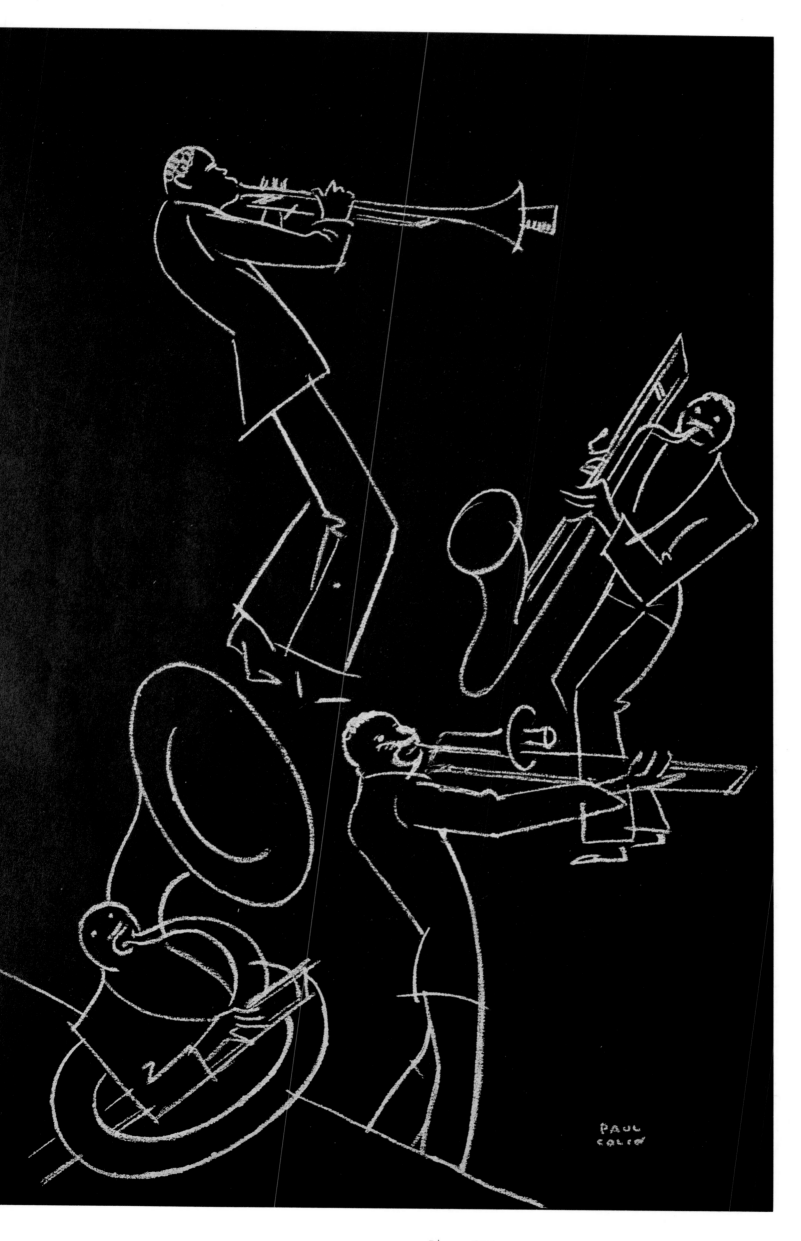

Plate 27

Plate 28

Plate 29

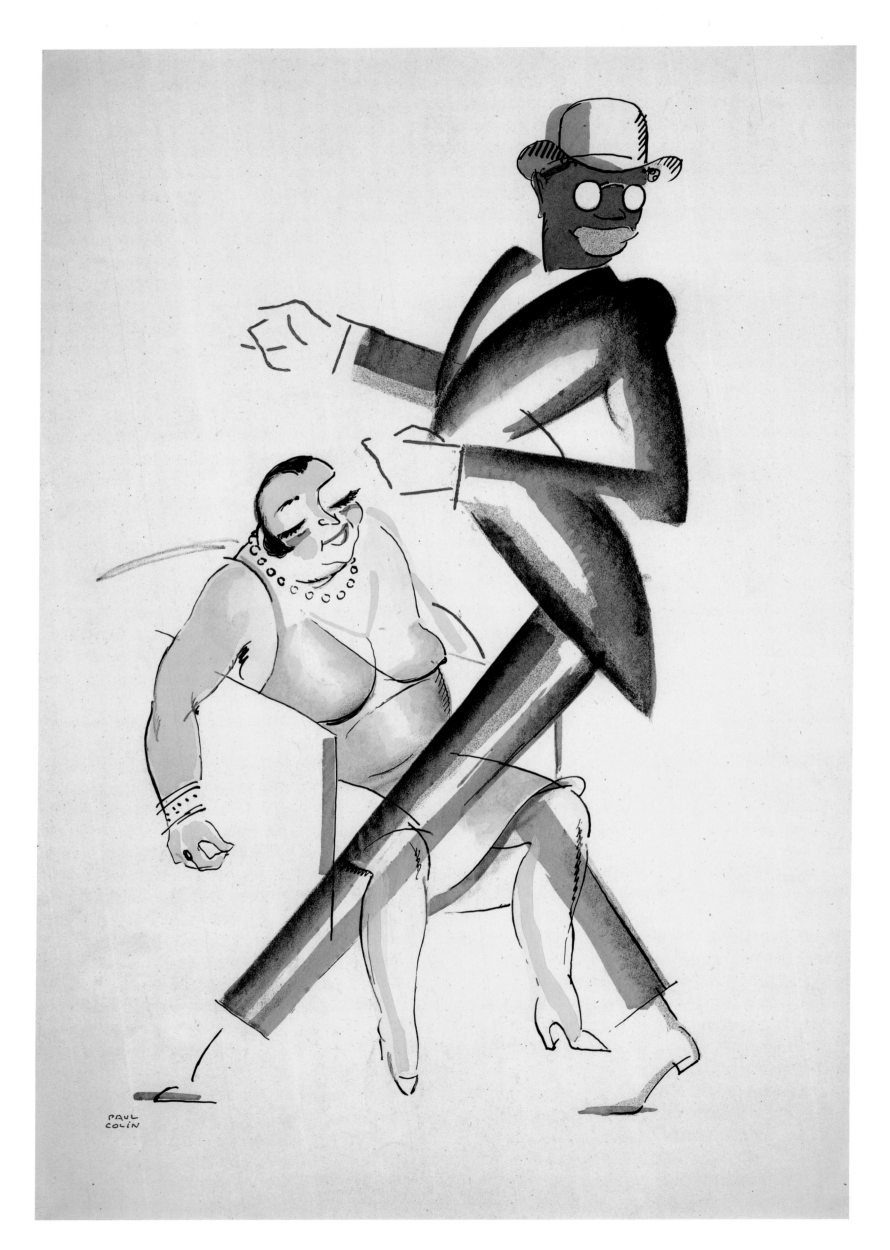

Plate 30

Plate 31

Plate 32

Plate 33

Plate 34

Plate 35

Plate 36

Plate 37

Plate 38

Plate 39

Plate 40

Plate 41

Plate 42

Plate 43

Plate 44

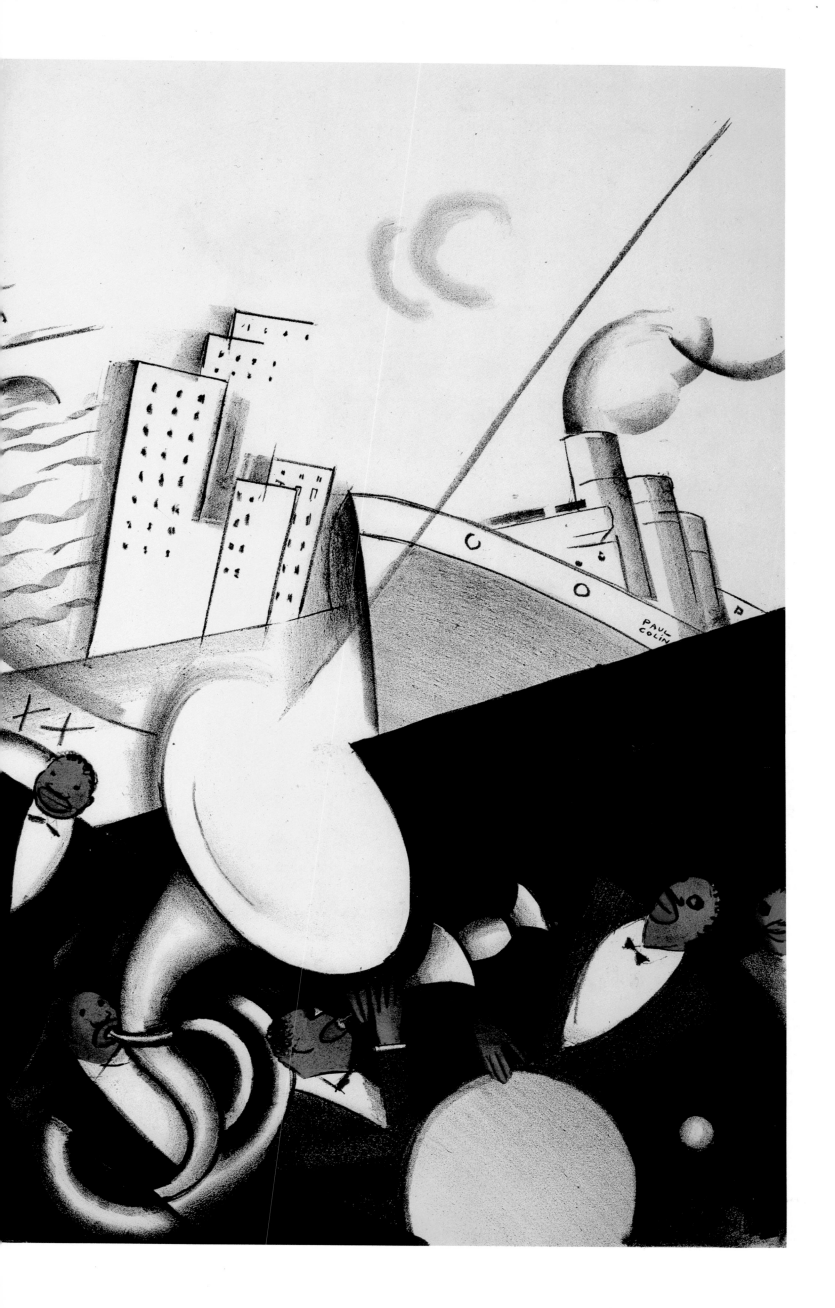

Adelaide Hall

PAUL
COLIN

Plate 45

TRANSLATION OF PREFACE BY RIP

I do not believe it is fair to hold Paul COLIN, recognized portraitist of Empress Josephine Baker, responsible for the Charlestonesque epidemic—indeed Charentonesque epidemic—which swooped down on Paris and its suburbs two years ago. In fact the *vomito negro* that infects our walls made its appearance well before they became covered with effigies glorifying the famous black star. For, since the armistice, Parisians stricken with Negropathy began obeying Uncle Tom's ukase.

Negroes in Africa, whose forebears were promoted slaves in America, dreamed one day of reducing Europe into slavery in turn. Therefore, they got on the road, traveling with only an extra shirt and a saxophone for baggage. They disembarked two by two, three by three, Kaffir by Kaffir. They invaded, Fulani by Fulani, the old continent and, if we can believe the Havas Travel Agency, they headed for Paris.

From then on we adopted their customs, we learned their dances. We vied at Negrifying ourselves.

At the Chatham Bar, which has become a branch for the Bahr-el-Ghazal, you can see gentlemen conscientiously blackening themselves. Over tea at the C(h)arl(es)ton, you can hear hens (Sudanese, no doubt) whispering mysteriously, "My Coco, my Coco."

From (Ivory) Penteco(a)st to Toussaint [All Saints' Day] (L'Ouverture) there were only Negro dances, Negro orchestras, Negro festivals, Negro balls, exhibitions of Negro art.

There was the Congo show.

At that time Mr. Solomon Reinach declared Mrs. Jane Cheirel rigorously Hottentot. Everyone was crazy for Pola Negri. The Baedecker Guide for foreigners visiting our capital was replaced by the Baker Guide. And every woman in Paris demanded heliotherapy to turn her white skin into boiled leather.

And it was at the Canni-bal(l) of the Countess d'Iguidi that someone took it upon himself to propose to the Académie française a poet who speaks *petit nègre* [broken French]: Mr. Paul Valéry.

The appearance of the great Josephine's frenetic rear end marked the apex of the TUMULTE NOIR and led to the final attack.

The Black Bottom dance was in some way the *delirium tremens* of Negromania. Thank God, the epidemic seems to be subsiding. The craze tends to be more localized. The cases of wild madness are decreasing. Fewer old ladies are dying from dancing the Charleston. And the convulsionaries of tropical choreography are more rare.

Just have a seat. This too shall pass.

Paul Colin therefore was right to record for future generations this period of national, secular, and obligatory lunacy. Under his incisive pencil, which is both scalpel and lancet, these plates of Life in Paris from 1918 to 1928 [sic] seem intended for some Dupuytren Museum [surgical museum].

The piercing art of Paul Colin, its schematic stylization rooted in a rigorous knowledge of drawing, and its incredible sense of movement will make it possible for future ballerinas to reconstruct modern dances, just as we have been able to rediscover steps honoring the Panatheneans from Greek vase paintings.

And the ballerinas of the future will be directed immediately to a special clinic at the Dépôt.

RIP

SELECTED BIBLIOGRAPHY

BAKER, Jean-Claude, and Chris CHASE. *Josephine: The Hungry Heart*. New York: Random House, 1993.

BAKER, Josephine. *Les Mémoires de Joséphine Baker*. Paris: KRA, 1927.

————. *Les Mémoires de Joséphine Baker recueillis et adaptés par Marcel Sauvage*. Paris: Editions Correa, 1949.

BLAKE, Jody. *"Le tumulte noir:* Modernist Art and Popular Entertainment in Jazz-Age Paris, 1900–1930." Ph.D. diss., University of Delaware, 1992.

COLIN, Paul. *La Croûte (Souvenirs)*. Paris: La Table Ronde, 1957.

COVARRUBIAS, Miguel. *Negro Drawings*. New York and London: Alfred A. Knopf, 1927.

COX, Beverly, and Denna Jones ANDERSON. *Miguel Covarrubias Caricatures*. Exhibition catalogue, Washington, D.C., National Portrait Gallery, 16 November 1984–13 January 1985. Washington, D. C.: Smithsonian Institution Press, 1985.

ERBSTEIN-THOMÉ, Marguerite. *Paul Colin, le magicien des années folles*. Laxou: Editions de l'est, 1994.

EMERY, Lynn Fauley. *Black Dance in the United States from 1619 to 1970*. New York: Dance Horizons, 1980.

FABRE, Michel. *From Harlem to Paris: Black American Writers in France, 1840–1980*. Urbana and Chicago: University of Illinois Press, 1991.

HAMMOND, Bryan, and Patrick O'CONNOR. *Josephine Baker*. London: Jonathan Cape, 1988.

Miguel Covarrubias: Homenaje. Mexico City: Centro Cultural/Arte Contemporáneo and Editorial MOP, 1987.

NAVARRETE, Sylvia. *Miguel Covarrubias: Artista y explorador*. Galería, colección de arte mexicano. Mexico City: Dirección General de Publicaciones del Consejo Nacional para la Cultura y las Artes and Ediciones Era, 1993.

Paul Colin et les spectacles. Exhibition catalogue, Nancy, Musée des Beaux-Arts, 2 May–31 July 1994. Nancy: Musée des Beaux-Arts, 1994.

ROSE, Phyllis. *Jazz Cleopatra: Josephine Baker in Her Time*. New York, London, Toronto, Sydney, Auckland: Doubleday, 1989.

RUBIN, William, ed. *"Primitivism" in 20th Century Art: Affinity of the Tribal and the Modern*. 2 vols. New York: The Museum of Modern Art, 1984.

STOVALL, Tyler. *Paris noir: African Americans in the City of Light*. Boston and New York: Houghton Mifflin Company, 1996.

WEILL, Alain, and Jack RENNERT. *Paul Colin, affichiste*. Paris: Editions Denoël, 1989.

INDEX

Numbers following entries refer to page numbers unless otherwise specified. Page numbers in *italic* type refer to illustrations. Plates refer to Paul Colin's illustrations for *Le Tumulte Noir*. "JB" stands for "Josephine Baker."